"For the power
power
is in them..."

"For the power is in them..."

MORMON MUSINGS

Neal A. Maxwell

Published by
DESERET BOOK COMPANY
Salt Lake City, Utah
1973

Library of Congress Catalog Card No. 70-120731
SBN No. 87747-432-X

Copyright 1970
by
Deseret Book Company

Second Printing 1973

Lithographed by

DESERET PRESS

in the United States of America

DEDICATION:

To the young Mormons . . . whose stirrings and thrust often stem from their twin visions of a world marching blindly toward Armageddon and a world in which, if we will, we can "invent" a future worthy of millenarian dreams.

. . .and whose desire to count for something on the scales of action finds them ripe with promise—as were David and Joseph in their time, bright and fashioned out of a rich heritage. Today's youth must make their choices as did these two predecessors: either achievement, followed by sensual use of status and power which was blind to rightness in relationships with man and God; or, achievement, followed by a deserved flow of trust from man and God which remained inviolate, gracefully and under pressure.

With confidence in them . . . that they will discover, again and again, that the only formula for lasting human betterment came from Him who hailed from a small, despised town, came to his own "and his own received Him not," who endured the "awful arithmetic" of an atonement He could have avoided, in order to do his divine duty. May the young Mormons keep their rendezvous with destiny.

With the hope that the rest of us . . . will meanwhile welcome the infusion of idealism from youth, realizing that millenarianism is not a mutation in Mormonism, but rather the mainstream. It is not our task to "put it down," but to help the young to develop a partnership with God in bringing it to pass.

INTRODUCTION

Verily I say, men should be anxiously engaged in a good cause, and do many things of their own free will, and bring to pass much righteousness;

For the power is in them, wherein they are agents unto themselves. And inasmuch as men do good they shall in no wise lose their reward.

D&C 58:27-28

For a rising generation seemingly determined to be "anxiously engaged" as "idealists without illusions" in a time when the use of power in all forms is accentuated, the thoughts in this spare volume stress sharing the untapped resources and the spiritual power within each of us.

The reflections risked are those of a believer who views the world through "an eye of faith." The musings are especially for those who "see not" yet, but who, if they will "dispute not, because (they) see not," will find that the interplay of the gospel and life will soon permit them to "witness for themselves" that the gospel is a constellation of correct principles without which there can be no happiness here and no exaltation in the world to come. Someday we will truly see with our eyes those things we have previously seen only "with an eye of faith." Like the ancients who so lived and prevailed "and they were glad," we, too, can rejoice fully, then and there.

A "wise servant" does not need to be commanded "in all things," for in "many things" men can "bring to pass much righteousness, for the power is in them."

These brief disclosures are shaped in that spirit and with that hope.

—Neal A. Maxwell

"For the power is in them . . ."

Man has made remarkable progress in the physical and biological sciences because he has discovered the universal laws which underlie the natural order. By applying those laws, man has "broken" the genetic code, landed on the moon, produced a whole new world of throbbing computers with their infinite possibilities, and work is proceeding on artifical hearts, kidneys, and eyes. Significantly, no one has seen a gene, nor, indeed many of the other things on which assumptions are based. But science has been willing to work on the "evidence of things not seen which are true."

Our failures in the areas of behavioral and social sciences, however, are so gross that it suggests we have not yet discovered the universal laws which underlie our spiritual order, or that we chronically fail to apply them. As a result, according to one historian, this planet has been war-free only 300-plus years out of 3400 years of recorded history. We now face massive problems of air and stream pollution. Our public welfare programs won't work and appear counter-productive. Our rising affluence has been gutted by rising crime. Our rising economic security for most is undercut by the rising use of drugs to escape from an economic Eden gone awry.

There is, therefore, a spiritual ecology in which the laws and principles enunciated by Jesus Christ are intertwined. Just as the people of the Church need each other in order to grow, gospel principles need each other in order to be fully effective. It was Chesterton who observed that the doctrines of Christ, when they are isolated from each other, can go wild. The master ecology which inter-

1

relates and intertwines these laws is what man must recognize and apply, if we want human happiness here and now. When we violate this spiritual ecology which pertains to human nature, we pay the consequences just as surely as when we violate the order of nature.

Strip-mining scars the landscape, causes floods, and leaves an economic emptiness which haunts the coming generations. Similarly, unchastity leaves terrible scars, brings floods of tears and anguish, and leaves a moral emptiness. Significantly, both strip-mining and unchastity rest on a life-style which partakes of an "eat, drink, and by merry" philosophy—gouge and grab now without regard to the consequences! Both strip-mining and unchastity violate the spirit of stewardship over our planet and over person. In such context, birth control pills are not a substitute for discipline. As one author observed, the coming of the pill may simply substitute a "copulation explosion for a population explosion."

The sense of rage, degradation, and despair experienced by many of the hundreds of Japanese young men and women sired by American servicemen and then abandoned is further testimony to the harsh consequences we experience, individually and socially, when the law of chastity is broken.

The principle of work is also fundamental to spiritual ecology. We shall come to know that work is a spiritual necessity, even if the time comes when it is not an economic necessity.

We can scarcely solve the problem of aid to dependent children unless fathers are willing to stand at the head of their households, leading them and loving them, rather than abandoning them.

The gospel insights about the importance of love at home are underscored by the terrible events of our time in which twisted men have acted out their hostility on mankind because there was no love at home or in their marriage.

The awful arithmetic of alcoholism is such, that while we have expressed much anguish, and rightly so, over the 40,000 men killed in Vietnam in the last nine years, we fail to realize that during that same period of time nearly half a million of our citizens were killed on American highways and nearly 250,000 of these fatalities involved alcohol. Children who are beaten by alcoholic parents have such little chance to lead any kind of normal life that we are right to be concerned about this problem. When we violate spiritual ecology we pay a price just as surely as when we pollute our sources of water.

Spiritual ecology also attests to the importance of the gospel teachings which point up the reality of our brotherhood with all of those who live on this planet. It is not a mere biological brotherhood in which we share circumstances, temporarily, only to have our relationships snuffed out; it is a brotherhood that makes real demands on us in terms of love, candor, and service in the context of friendships that will last millions of years—forever!

The real fatherhood of God is a further basic factor in the spiritual ecology affecting all living systems on this earth. Real fatherhood helps us to see that God is not

3

simply a "life force," nor is God, as C.S. Lewis so aptly puts it, a kindly "grandfather," but rather a Loving Father who will not have us "take happiness in sin."

In a host of ways, then, social and political problems of our time lend themselves to solution only when we apply to them the teachings of Jesus! Until and when we do, the disparity between our scientific progress and our spiritual progress will continue to haunt us. Indeed, in an age of many causes, we need to remember that Jesus "advocateth the cause of the children of men"—both in connection with our "here and now" problems and prepared us for the "there and then" of eternity.

Too often in our home, at work, and even in the Church we practice one-way communication instead of two-way communication with resulting impasses in relationships. A case study in the scriptures of such an impasse occurs between Moroni and Pahoran (Alma, Chapter 60). In a time of great turbulence, Moroni feels the central government which is presided over by Pahoran is letting him down. He accuses Pahoran and his colleagues of "being in a state of thoughtless stupor" and of "exceeding great neglect" of their duties. He exhorts them to be "up and doing." Because there has not been two-way communication, Moroni does not realize that Pahoran has his own problems, having been driven from the capital. Pahoran finally replies to Moroni—without anger—despite the fact that Moroni was angry with him. Once two-way communication was established, Moroni's stereotype notions about the failures at "headquarters" were dissolved and Moroni comes to Pahoran's aid.

Often in life we believe the worst of each other in the absence of adequate information and under the stress and strain of circumstances. Our imagination hardens our view of circumstances and even conjures up images of failures on the part of others which either have not happened at all, or for which there is good reason.

We are so close to something of great significance that is happening in our American society, that we seem to miss one of the tragic consequences of our increased size, complexity, and dependency! As size, complexity and dependency have increased, there has been a corresponding increase in the vulnerability of society to little people and little things that can go wrong (a tiny electrical part mulfunctions causing a blackout on the East Coast, a strike of garbagemen almost paralyzes New York City). Just as the Apollo 7 contained five million individual parts, only one of which had to malfunction to cause a crisis, our American society has over 200 million "parts," and one or a small number of those individuals can cause a serious crisis.

One wild or ill individual at anytime in history has been able, of course, to inflict his hostilities on a few others, but he could scarcely cripple or wipe out a city so easily. Thus, the sick or the wild among us have increased their impact within our system.

One almost hates to speak of these things because

acknowledging them makes us wonder if mere mention will trigger the madness and the deed.

Our basic choices appear to be two-fold in this situation: We will have to devote more and more of our society's resources to protecting the vital parts of our system, such as our water supplies, etc., while acknowledging, at the same time, that any system of protection can be beaten; *or* we can use our resources and our judgment in loving and caring for our neighbors in such a way that we make them less likely to bring disaster upon us all. Small towns have often been panned in American novels, but the village incompetent of yesteryear was usually cared for pretty well; at least allowances were made for him, which are not replicated in the modern metropolis. Our circles of effective love do not overlap in a modern city; our circles do not even touch sometimes, stranding souls who hunger for attention and love. The Church can both enlarge and bring our circles together, so that no one is left "outside."

When I hear the phrase, "Do your own thing," I am ambivalent because it conveys two distinctly different impressions to me. First, it suggests the value and worth of each individual and the integrity and importance of what he does best to contribute to others. I can support that concept. But when I think "do your own thing" means that each of us should be "monastic" in doing our thing without concern for the needs of our whole society, I must disagree. There are some problems that cannot be solved unless people enlarge their own circle of concern in order to meet the common challenge.

It has been rightly said that any number multiplied by zero is zero. It is equally apropos to suggest that any number multiplied only by one is no larger than the original number; some problems require good men to "multiply" themselves and their impact so that the "sum" of social or spiritual action is more adequate. The Church can help us to "magnify" our otherwise solitary sums.

The blend of the human tendency to escape from challenges and of the organizational tendency to focus on facade can, at least on an individual basis, make the gospel something we merely "talk" about instead of "do". Reaffirmation, clarification, and repetition are all vital in any teaching and learning situation; but the failure to connect the teaching of the gospel with real life can make gospel discussion a kind of intellectual "cat's cradle," to be reshaped and passed back and forth. When this happens, it can give participants a sense of false security as a result of their playing the conversational game well—even though their behavior remains unchanged in relation to the challenges of the gospel.

Somewhere between the extreme of "cat's cradle" classrooms and the other extreme of hypertense, activist teachers (who do not understand the role of contemplation, reflection, and worship and who would empty the classrooms of the Church and have us all march off heedlessly to become involved) there is a golden mean wherein

7

teaching is outcome-oriented, in which teaching makes fresh demands of us with our consent—a kind of teaching which brings life and lessons together. Such teaching generates faith which moves us to productive action in behalf of others because the gospel is true. And we continue to know that it is true because we constantly witness it working!

It is clear that even when we let our light shine without ostentation and with no thought of doing deeds "to be seen of men," there still can arise situations in which our example —per se—goads others. Nephi's righteousness and his father's frequent citations of Nephi's spiritual superiority to his older brothers did not go down well with Laman or Lemuel, (and Lemuel was clearly Laman's unwavering psychological satellite. See 1 Nephi 3:28.)

That others may be so offended is not reason for us to reduce such righteousness as we have, of course, but awareness of this irony is a reminder for us to be sensitive to the needs and feelings of others who can be greatly inflamed with resentment. The tale of Aristides the Just is ancient Greece is another reminder of this paradox.

Aristides encountered an illiterate citizen who was struggling to make out his ostrakon (the periodic way in which ancient Greeks could, with sufficient "votes," exile an offending countryman). When Aristides inquired as to whether or not he could help this man mark his ostrakon, the man said yes and asked, not knowing who his helper was, to have the name of Aristides put on the "ballot" as deserving of ostracism. Aristides, wisely seeking feedback, still did not identify himself but asked why the man wished this fate upon Aristides. The man said it was because he had grown tired of hearing incessantly how noble and how just Aristides was. There was, apparently, an intrinsic resentment of Aristides' image of nobility.

It is not necessary to be able to account for, or to analyze, all the psychological variables involved in such situations in order to know that in human affairs the "Aristides factor" often does operate. It is a sensitive leader who is aware of how he may thus have impact on others, and who can make allowances for this factor without compromising his basic life stance.

Man is acquiring a new respect—almost too late—for the wondrous order and ecology of nature, in which the relationships of organisms and their environments reflect natural cycles and rhythm. The pollution of our atmosphere and streams, the denigration of nature's mountain wonders, and the general loss of man's direct interface with nature (which may be greater a spiritual need than we of the asphalt age realize) have suddenly shown us, more clearly than many of us have ever known before, that the order of nature is violated at our peril, and that man may not walk the earth with interruptional impunity. Man's task of establishing dominion over the earth is not to be achieved by arbitrarily imposing his will on his environment, but by acting in harmony with law.

Neal A. Maxwell

This concern with man's developing a more harmonious relationship with nature by abiding by its physical laws is timely and legitimate. When we interrupt or destroy the larger ecology of man's relationship to God and to his fellowmen, we are violating transcendental laws that are as immutable and as inevitable as those breeched laws of nature for which we now beginning to pay a terrible price. (Later installments will be even more severe.) That we do not fully understand these transcendental spiritual laws neither excuses us from learning of them, nor excuses us from their harsh consequences when we violate them.

We do not know, for instance, all of God's reasons for requiring us to be chaste. We can make sociological guesses, we can see the sadness of history—individual and cultural—when sex satiates a society as it did Sodom. We know from the Book of Mormon that in circumstances of gross unchastity "many hearts died, pierced with deep wounds."

While we do not know fully what the underlying rationale for chastity is, we certainly know enough to obey. A spiritual ecology, therefore, underlies our need to forgive, our need to pray, etc. As man more and more understands the physical laws that bind us all, it is cause for great wonder. When the ecology of spiritual laws is finally and fully understood, the awe will be even greater because of their simplicity, consistency, and inviolability.

Regarding our occasional hypertension in Church activity, in which too often we don't have time for each other except as functions, one is driven to ask, "If we really believe in eternity, why are we in such a hurry? And why are we too busy for things that would be appropriate for those who have the special perspective of the Gospel?"

As is true of all Jesus' teachings (with their possibilities for multiple learning and insights,) the incident with Mary and Martha (Luke 10:38-42) affords a view of an important leadership and life principle at work. For those of us who are "cumbered" and who suffer from Martha-like anxiety, Jesus urges us to be more thoughtful about choosing "that good part" in human relationships that will not "be taken" away from us. Being "careful" and "troubled about many things" can reflect devotion to duty to be sure; but a devotion which is so inverted that those things which matter most are at the mercy of things of this world may be more common than we think.

Life situations and leadership situations often present us with Mary versus Martha type choices in terms of how we spend our time and the priority we assign to the tasks on our "agenda" of action. Mary "heard his word", exploiting a unique, one-time opportunity to learn from the Master. Martha had no doubt served hundreds of meals before and would serve hundreds after Jesus' visit. With our associates, partners, and children in a fleeting mortality—do we tend to make Martha or Mary choices?

How many of us have privately identified, at least at first blush, not only with Martha but also with the stay-at-home brother of the prodigal son? If so, some introspection

11

may be useful. Do we feel put upon at times, as Martha must have done, in busy situations in which nobody appears to appreciate what we are doing and others seem heedless of the many tasks that must be done? Do we feel the prodigals get attention that really should be ours, and also that they seem to have their cake and eat it, too? There are even deeper implications, but the thrust of these implications may be our inability to love. For true love can help us to see what is most needed and what is most important. And true love can gladly and spontaneously respond when others come to their senses. Those of us who "are in the field," who hear the sounds of rejoicing, can stay outside and withhold our warmth. But if it is our Father's quiet respect we really want (since we have his love) and not the attention-getting of receiving "a fatted calf," we will do better not to require our Father or his servants to come out and entreat us. For while our loyalty to Him is not at issue, our degree of maturity is. It is as if, child-like, we demand "equal time" and attention, and our Father says "If it is reassurance you need, you shall have it; but would that you were more ready for the full burdens of leadership."

Besides, few of us live so well that we are "ever with" Father. Most of us have experienced the pain that preceeds the joys of "homecomings." And even though our "home-comings" are quiet, and even though we were not in a "far country"—we were glad to know we would be "welcome!"

* * * * * *

"For the power is in them . . ."

One can be authoritative without being authoritarian; one can command respect without "commanding" others. These points should be borne in mind in an age when there is a flight from authority, a reluctance to over-see and to direct others. However much romance and psychological respite there are in the notion of everybody "doing his own thing," we must realize that the social sum of everybody's doing his "own thing" does not add up to an effective agenda of action to solve society's pressing problems.

When one's authority is properly derived (democratically in the case of secular situations or by priesthood channel in the Church), no apologies are necessary. Reluctance to lead is really a mild form of renunciation, whether the reluctance stems from fear of failure, from fear that our peers will withdraw their acceptance of us, or from ambivalence about the task which the leader must undertake. We have written and warned so much about power hungry leaders that we may have glorified the suicidal "march of the lemmings" as a leader-follower style.

In the din of youthful dissent—so much of which is tragically violent, crazed, and irrational—we who are older would do well to ponder some of the responsible concerns voiced by at least the thinking, responsible, and rational young. They find our society too hurried and too intense; they see our social institutions and programs too preoccupied with procedures and too highly structured to be

13

responsive to certain basic, human needs. They see us as too materialistic; they see too many things as irrelevant. While it would be easier to listen to them if there were no shouting and irresponsible dissenters, and while it would be easier to establish two-way communication if young critics would prescribe not just describe, nevertheless, some of what they say is at least a faint echo of earlier valid criticisms about hypocrisy, rigidity, and preoccupation with status in another society. The scribes, Pharisees, and hypocrites were denounced because they: "devoured widow's houses"; prayed often in pious "pretence"; "omitted the weightier matters of the law" (judgment, the love of God, mercy, and faith); appeared clean on the "outside" but within were full of "extortion and excess"; and loved "salutations" and "chief seats" in the "uppermost places".

Clearly, those in power have special responsibilities, and when they go wrong how much misery men suffer; or, in the words of Mosiah, ". . .how much iniquity doth one wicked king cause to be committed, yea, and what great destruction!"

Of course, current criticisms lack the accuracy and precision of Jesus' divine discernment, and especially the Master's prescriptive powers. But if we can listen for validity rather than being aggravated by volume, if we can be discerning rather than being disturbed because of the decibel level of dissent, we will see there are reasons to be concerned. The outward forms and procedures of society in the meridian of time were often as irrelevant as they were intense, in contrast to a Jesus who was racing the clock but who still found time somehow to respond to the spontaneous touch, petition, or request. Jesus' insightful comment about the correlation between where a man's heart is and where his treasure is, is still index to the value system of an individual or a society. The Old Testament warnings about the greedy poor and the rich who "neglected the poor and needy" and the warnings to ancient Israel about the virus of cultural arrogance are still worth pondering.

If it is true—as critics have suggested—that the young will assail adults on precisely those issues or problems with which adults have had the least success or about which they have displayed the least interest (even though their achievements in other areas have been significant), perhaps there is subtle purpose in giving some advance attention to those sectors of our society which are most vulnerable—since the young must meet their own Goliaths by the appointment of time. In any event, in such a situation, it does us little good to take the young on tours of the "Maginot Lines" we have built, if they sense that we do not see the massing forces that may sweep down upon us through a political or moral Belgium.

There is a real risk, however, in assuming that either the young or old—per se—see things with total clarity. C.S. Lewis warned us of how history shows both individuals and societies falling into the ironical trap of running about anxiously with fire extinguishers in times of flood.

15

Neal A. Maxwell

The only safety lies in the beautiful blend of concepts found in the gospel of Jesus Christ, for in these we see: a concern for the poor and a stress on the corrosiveness of envy and the duty and dignity of work; both a certitude about the need for authority and extensive warnings against exercising "unrighteous dominion." We see both persuasive teachings on the need for tolerance, love, and forgiveness and the need to assert the truth articulately, to stand by it rather than compromise the truth merely to make others feel good or comfortable (for Jesus had only to "put on" Pilate in order to go free, had only to "modify" his message to be accepted by Jerusalem's power structure). And we see both the goal "that every man should have an equal chance throughout all the land" and that rights are accompanied by corresponding responsibilities, since the social and political burdens "should come upon all the people that a very man might bear his part."

There is no more simple yet profound statement on the posture the generations who are separated in many ways by time and experience should adopt toward each other than the one found in the Book of Mormon (Mormon 9:31):

"Condemn me not because of mine imperfection, neither my father, because of his imperfection, neither them who have written before him; but rather give thanks unto God that he hath made manifest unto you our imperfections, that ye may learn to be more wise than we have been."

What more sublime statement could be made?—the

"outgoing" generations asking the "incoming" generation not to be harsh or too quick to judge—to profit from the mistakes of the past, but to be grateful to God for the opportunity to "learn to be more wise" than predecessors have been. Each of us leaves a "record" of memories for our friends and children to "read." Would that the "reading" could occur in the spirit of Moroni's counsel.

The young should be slower to condemn those who have preceded them, for they have not yet worn the "moccasins" of power and decision making. The old are urged to hope genuinely that their successors will be "more wise" than they have been. Obviously, the scripture relates to the major spiritual lessons about the failure and success of the societies described in the Book of Mormon stream of history; but the pithy verse, as scriptures often are, is replete with insight at several levels simultaneously.

The discouraging sweep of history appears so tragic and purposeless that it makes faith in God exceedingly difficult for some. Those who so hold are often sincere and articulate, and, truly, they are seldom "glad" to have concluded that there is no God.

Morris L. West, in *The Tower of Babel*, has one of his characters speak eloquently of the "tragedy of the human condition" in which man is "conceived without consent," "wrenched whimpering into an alien universe," in which man still preserves "the sacred illusion of immortality," in which "the believers were the lucky ones," since they have the gift of faith without which one is "thrust back on reason," which is "no key to the mystery and the paradox and the tragedy of the human condition." Elsewhere, good friends of mine have written that the tragic view of life is "the realization that man cannot control or even understand the forces that shape his life and order his death," and that if there is a Mind that understands, would not any such Mind that men could understand become sated at last with irony?"

Faith is a gift, of course, and reason, by itself, cannot lead man out of the apparent maze. Man does not understand the mind of God and his timetable; nor do we have his perspective. The gift of faith, then, often gives form to what has been called "tacit knowledge," that form of knowledge that lies just below the level of the individual's powers of articulation, which whispers things to him that are true but which are difficult to share and can seldom be put in persuasiave form for the ears of others. Nevertheless, without the gift of faith or the perspective-giving insights of the gospel, man's reason will sweep him into sadness and cynicism.

It is little wonder some individuals may never get any nearer to faith than to be "almost" persuaded. Our response to such individuals and their view of the human condition cannot be to give them saccharine, ritualistic reassurances or to cavalierly dismiss their dismay. Without the perspective of the gospel, without the critical data God has shared with us about man and the universe, life for us, too, would be a maze without a clue, a brief encounter with just enough joy to foreshadow what might be, but which wouldn't be —because nothingness would come crashing in.

It is natural for cynicism to flow from such foreboding; it is even natural for such views of the pointlessness of life to produce in some—not all—the modern equivalent of "eat, drink, and be merry." The lines from the song in "Kismet" ("Princes come. . .Princes go. . .an hour of pomp and show") seem to suggest a senseless history. But for a believer, history is also senseless—senseless to the things of God. Man has gone awry from want of the perspective of the gospel as it tells us of the purpose of life. Yet how can life be a growth experience if God suspends all the opposition, if he interrupts the experience with its pain and paradoxes? Life is an "open-book" exam, but the problem is that most of the students don't have the "book", or refuse to open it—a fact that ought to spur us on as Church members to share the gospel more widely so that life would be meaningful for more people.

In his agony after his wife's death C.S. Lewis noted how God's plan placed Him in the role of the surgeon who must continue the operation against a patients protests, in full view of his pain, else "all the pain up to that point would. . . [be] useless."* Once we all knew this, and accepted it. God is being true to the promises He made to the patient before

*C.S. Lewis, *A Grief Observed.*

the events of the "operating room"—where our pleadings to stop must go unheeded—because of an irrevocable decision we made when we knew before and agreed to be "wrenched whimpering into an alien universe."

The chiliast, one who believes in a second coming of Christ that will usher in a millenial reign, has special challenges in reading signs. First, he is urged to notice lest he be caught unawares. Second, he must be aware of how many false readings and alarms there have been in bygone days, even by the faithful. For instance, has any age had more "wonders in the sky" than ours, with satellites and journeys to the moon? Has any generation seen such ominous "vapors of smoke" as ours with its mushroom clouds over the pathetic pyres of Hiroshima and Nagasaki? Yet there is "more to come." Our task is to react and to notice without overreacting, to let life go forward without slipping into the heedlessness of those in the days of Noah. It has been asked, and well it might be, how many of us would have jeered, or at least been privately amused, by the sight of Noah building his ark. Presumably, the laughter and the heedlessness continued until it began to rain-and kept raining! How wet some people must have been before Noah's ark suddenly seemed the only sane act in an insane, bewildering situation! To ponder signs without becoming paranoid, to be aware without frantically matching current events with expectations, using energy that should be spent in other ways—these are our tasks.

"For the power is in them . . ."

Helen Hayes calls them "intellectual hemlines," but by whatever name they are called, each generation seems to have both its special ways of acting out its break with tradition and its morality fads. God's morality has always been inclusive of both "the weightier matter of the law" and the lesser things which still should not be "left undone." It is man who seized upon some segment of morality; it is man who seeks to "specialize"—as if we could invoke a narrower morality! Preoccupation with contemporary social challenges is both good and natural, but to question the morality or faith of members who do not seem as alarmed about a particular cause or as passionate about a certain problem as we are is unwise. This is reminiscent of those who in past decades measured morality largely by compliance with the Word of Widom rather than by how chaste they were or how well they loved their neighbors. God has never ceased to be interested in free agency and all threats to it (of any kind), neither has he lost his interest in human health—nor in chastity. Manhood is measured by total morality and not by the latest litmus paper morality tests that some would apply to us as a sole and ultimate test of our devotion to the Kingdom.

It is a task of the Church to avoid tying to political movements, even though these may sincerely mirror some similar concerns. Resisting alliances with groups or movements regardless of their place along the political spectrum is not done out of pride or unfriendliness, but because of

Neal A. Maxwell

our responsibility to be carriers of a divine message is so important that we must not compromise that message by offending those who might heed it if its light could shine forth unobstructed by the shadow of any mortal alliances. The Church and its members can cooperate in seeing that the community chores are done without letting others use or exploit us—without unconsciously finding ourselves marching to the cadence of a cause which is called by other voices for other purposes.

President Harold B. Lee has called our attention to the phrase "past feeling" which is used several places in the scriptures. In Ephesians, Paul links it to lasciviousness that apparently so sated its victims that they sought "uncleanness with greediness." Moroni used the same two words to describe a decaying society which was "without civilization," "without order and without mercy," and in which people had "lost their love, one towards another." Insensate, this society saw violence, gross immorality, brutality and all kinds of "kamikaze" behavior. Nephi used the same concept in his earlier lamentation about his brothers' inability to heed the urgings of the Spirit because they were "past feeling." The common thread is obvious: the inevitable dulling of our capacity to feel renders us impervious to conscience, to the needs of others, and to insights both intellectual and spiritual. Such imperceptivity, like alcoholism, apparently reaches a stage where the will can no longer enforce itself upon our impulses.

"For the power is in them . . ."

It is often asked, "Where are the great Mormon painters, sculptors, artists, etc.?" It is presumptive for one with such "middlebrow" tastes to attempt a response, but perhaps a "middlebrow" has some special clinical detachment. For instance, since Church members now constitute about .001% of the world's population, it is not statistically likely that we will have any Michaelangelos or Beethovens— let alone several.

Perhaps, some say, there is reason to expect us to overproduce so that we account for at least a few blips on the cultural radar screen. But I know of no scriptural promise that suggests such overproduction. But it is often said, shouldn't we at least "try harder?" Perhaps, yet the commitment to family and the chores of the Kingdom mitigate against the harsh, unrelenting disciplines that even genius requires.

There appears, however, to be no written hostility to the arts, though there may be and probably are attitudinal deterrents among individual members. In fact, there is scriptural affirmation: "If there is anything virtuous, lovely, or of good report, or praiseworthy, we seek after these things." The rising generation of bright, talented young Church members may give us both "models" or artists who can do their home teaching and still play in Carnegie Hall. Meanwhile, a middle brow question: Is there a divine music or art? If so, the Church ought to reflect it and even to originate some of it. But does God really have a favorite school of painting, or musical composition? Or are such things a matter of preference, not principle? "There is

23

beauty all around" and "we seek after these things." We clearly have an affirmative obligation to appreciate and to see and, presumably, to create as best a small culture can.

In reflecting on C.S. Lewis' observations about how those very doctrines of the gospel which presently seem most puzzling to us—or even the least persuasive—may be the very concepts we most need in our lives and may be the very concepts we need to discover if our lives are to have wholeness, one is struck by how much symmetry there is in the fullness of the gospel. This fullness can help us: to balance the pervasive, relentless demands of "now" and "here" with the perspective of eternity's "there" and "then"; to ride out the fads and keep our heads amidst the seismic social peaks and valleys; to accept new adventures that require us to leave our comfortable nests in which there would otherwise be an avoidance of adventure with its threat of new experience. Lewis also notes how events and circumstances can truly confirm a doctrine which we have accepted intellectually but which suddenly "blossoms" into reality, giving beauty and strength to our lives. This observation suggests that teachings may not meet up with confirming experience till later.

Parents and teachers—to shift the metaphor—are planting little intellectual time bombs that will be set off by certain pressures of circumstance and human chemistry. This perspective ought to give teachers and parents reason to reflect on the nature of their teaching investment. The parental portfolio needs balance between teaching on current matters and the teaching whose dividends will be deferred till a time when they will be much needed—in four years or in a decade.

How wonderful it is to see those whose sense of humor includes the capacity to see themselves and their frailties laughingly—not in the chronic, self-deprecating, biting way. Those who can see themselves and their incongruities with smiles (not sarcasm) suggest to the rest of us that they have an inner security, and this encourages the rest of us to take heart in a world in which too many of us are much too serious about ourselves and in which too much of the laughter is nervous laughter.

La Rochefoucauld gave us a marvelous figure: "There goes another beautiful theory about to be murdered by a brutal gang of facts." The "school" of mortality we are in is situated on a beautiful "campus," but it is, fortunately, not so detached from reality that we can theorize endlessly and painlessly. Harsh realities and the cares of the world take their toll and there is no way to stay in the sandpile. Our theories and ideas are finally put to the test; and while the laboratory of life will confront us with many disappointments, it will also offer us the excitement of achievements through confirmation and discovery. The gospel is the only constellation of concepts which is illusion-free.

Not only did Jesus underline the primacy of love as a gospel concept, but he gave us criteria to measure our progress in developing our capacity to love: Do we love our enemies? Do we do good to them which hate us? Do we pray for those who have despitefully used us? Can we love those who falsely accuse us? (Reciprocated love is not enough, since "sinners also love those that love them.")

Using Paul's criteria from the 13th chapter of First Corinthians (Moffatt version):

If we really have love, we are "patient," "very kind," and "never rude."

If we really have love, we "make no parade" of our accomplishments.

If we really have love, we are "never resentful" and are "slow to expose" others.

Neither is true love "glad when others go wrong": love is "gladdened by goodness."

Each of us experiences difficulty: when he has been "used" or wrongly accused; when he is in competitive relationships; when he has done good (or tried to) and his acts or motives are nevertheless misunderstood; when his self-image is attacked; and when his love is unresponded to and unappreciated.

There is another factor worthy of mention. Just as football coach Vince Lombardi suggests, with reference to football, that "fatigue makes cowards of us all," there is the cowardice that comes when we are tired and physically spent, and when we suffer from what has been called "people fatigue."

"For the power is in them . . ."

While listening to a piano player in a restaurant in Weisbaden, Germany, I noticed how few of the diners paid him any heed. They no doubt appreciated his music, and dinner was more enjoyable because of his music, but there was little response or expression of appreciation. The young man playing the piano didn't seem to mind, however; he was playing for his own pleasure, in a sense, and his satisfaction had to come from inside—not from external responses that he had learned not to expect. This is symbolic of some aspects of life. That which we do that is good and fine often will not be noticed or responded to. We often use others as helpful functions without dignifying them as humans by responding to them or their helpful efforts. If we condition our "metabolism" of interpersonal relations to require large doses of recognition or constant response from others, we will be disappointed— as much as deserved praise and response are helpful and appreciated when they do come our way. Our need for response can become narcotic, and we may find that we do good things for the wrong reasons simply to elicit attention.

The aloneness of the atonement in its final hours symbolized how we must, at times, do what needs to be done, even if no mortal understands or appreciates what is being done. In fact, the atonement with its awful arithmetic (the billions who would benefit from the exquisite agony of Christ as he somehow bore thousands of sins for each of us) was *the last appreciated but most beneficial act in human history!*

27

We are all aware of man's poor peripheral vision in that his views are often narrow and heedless of what is going on on each side of him. Man's problem is often one of length of view, too. This poorness of perspective often produces wonderful and pathetic paradoxes: men who have been given the blessings of life by the grace of God, cry that life is senseless; men who have been given breath and voice by God, use the powers of speech to deny God's existence; men who have been given the capacity to feel exult so much in this gift that sensual things sublimate spiritual things; and some men who see our reaching out to distant places in our solar system conclude that this special planet is a random, unplanned mutant and refuse to connect the order of physical laws (that makes such journeys into space possible) with an Orderer. Yet, seeing this ingratitude of those who are without perspective should not cause us to make reflexive rejoinders to unbelievers. Rather, we, for our part, ought to contemplate how truly deep God's commitment to free agency must be, how truly deep (and unpossessive) his love for his children must be to allow us to err, to fail, to learn, and to grow. And how wonderful is his refusal to impose, by his power, a faith that otherwise seems to come so slowly and to so few when men are left free. Sensing, even on such a small scale, these divine commitments ought to help us to reflect them in our lives. If we are tempted to unwise responses because of our small-scale frustrations with those who are ungrateful, with those who misuse their gifts, lo, how much greater the sense of disappointment at the divine level is.

"For the power is in them . . ."

And yet his commitment to free agency remains intact, and his love, justice, and mercy continue even for those who defy their Father.

On an overnight train from Barcelona, while others slept, I was restless. The night sky was especially resplendent. It was during the same week that man first left his footprints on the moon. The overwhelming majesty of the universe suggested a major communication problem God has with man. Our limited, finite minds could not contain many answers even if God chose to give them to us. Moses was overcome following the panoramic presentation he received, saying in response to that sunburst of revelation "That man is nothing, which thing I never supposed." Living by faith, then, is not simply a test, but a necessity—until we are ready to receive more divine data. Meanwhile, we often go on asking God, as C.S. Lewis observed, questions even He cannot answer because they are the equivalent of: "How big is Yellow?" When we often can't frame the right question, and could not contain the answer if it were given, silence must be God's only response at times.

True religion reflects concern over our relationships with both God and man, since a violation of relationship on the human plane means a breech of a relationship with God, and vice versa. Joseph resisted the verbal caresses of Potiphar's wife and cited to her how wrong adultery would be in view of how much her husband trusted him,

Joseph, as overseer "over all that" Potiphar had. Joseph also said, ". . .How can I do this great wickedness, and sin against God?" Without a parallel concern over breeching our relationships with our Father, it is too easy to rationalize the impact of our behavior on our brothers. The prodigal son also showed this same awareness of moral obligations at the human and divine levels. When "he came to himself" he vowed to say to his Father, "I have sinned against heaven, *and* before thee." He did just this, and told his father of his sin against heaven "*and* in thy sight." John laid down the tightness of the correlation: "If a man say, I love God, and hateth his brother, he is a liar. . ."

Total morality must concern itself both with man's relationships with God and with his fellowmen. In Alma 27:27 we read of Church members of another age who ". . .were also distinguished for their zeal towards God, and *also* towards men; for they were perfectly honest and upright in all things. . ." These members looked upon the shedding of blood with "the greatest abhorrence," but they did not look upon death "with any degree of terror" because of their "views of Christ and the resurrection." The gentleness and intergrity that are borne of the perspective of the gospel are truly impressive when one sees them in others. In this fragment of history we see an impressive statement about an entire group who bore up under persecution in a time of tribulation without losing their love of God *and* man.

Our experiences with our fellowmen and the wonders of exchanging even finite love can increase our awe and wonder at God's capacity for perfect love, while experiencing God's love for us can increase the quality and constancy of our efforts to serve our fellowmen, his other children.

Man, at times, in his agony of disbelief, is like a passenger on a fast train which is headed toward the dark tunnel of death. He shouts at the sky out of his sense of tragedy, sees others on the train only as fleeting faces huddling together for warmth, the journey as pointless, the dark tunnel as inescapable and terminal, when actually, the train is "going home," and he is going to be with many of his fellow passengers forever.

It is clear that in some situations we can rely on the faith of others. The Book of Mormon prophet asked the king if he believed and the king said, "And if now thou sayest there is a God, Behold I will believe." The striplings "did not doubt" that their mothers knew the gospel was true. And, as we read in the Section 46 of the Doctrine and Covenants, "to some it is given by the Holy Ghost to know that Jesus Christ is the Son of God. . .to others it is given to believe on their words. . . ." The dark side of that coin, of course, is that doubts can be pooled, too, and anxieties shared with the wrong people so that this wilts such few tender sprouts of certitude as exist. The point is not that we should refuse to share our concerns, but that sincere doubters really seek for answers, while it is often the insincere doubter who wants to play. "Can you top this?" in a frenzy of doubt for doubt's sake.

Candor in the context of love (not that candor which is used to punish, to shock, or to role play) offers many advantages: it can provide more information for leaders and followers; it can give us feedback of both feelings and facts as to our individual impact on others and the merits of our ideas as seen by others; and it can help us avoid a repetition of errors. It can have a beneficial cathartic effect in that, having "levellled," a follower can avoid the guilt that can accompany the after-effects of silence when we know we should have spoken up; and the follower can also comply with a decision which has gone "against" him with the assurance that he tried and that his views were asserted. Such candor in the context of love is especially necessary in authoritarian organizations or situations.

Just as trust and love between individuals frees us to listen, human nature also makes it easier to listen to the "critic" who really loves that which he criticizes. My experience in the Church is that the devoted, committed member *is* listened to (he may not find his counsel followed, of course) because his caring (which underlines his complaint) manifests itself in specific ways which remove any doubts about his devotion. True, we can and should learn from our "enemies," and we ought to be able to' hear even the disaffected, but simply having authority does not produce such perfection in listening, and those who really wish to be heard instead of just venting their feelings would do well to make this allowance.

So many times, it has become clear in my own life, and in the lives of others I am close enough to be able to observe, that there are "a few" special people whose approval of us means a great deal. We really care about what "they" think. Though there are some "theys" who have the power to punish us or whom we care about out of fear, our concern is with those whose love, trust, and respect rightfully play an important role in our lives. The "theys" of trust have, therefore, a different interface with us and others. Note the diagrammatic analogy below:

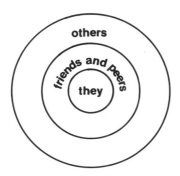

Our "theys" change often with the passage of time and changing environments, but reflecting on who our "theys" are can tell us much about ourselves, our values, and our sources of satisfaction. The "theys" needn't be status-ful individuals. In fact, the variety of our "theys" is a clue to the breadth of our lives. It is sobering to realize, too, that we are somebody's "they", whether or not we realize this or are ready to be such a reference individual.

Yet our "theys" ought to be provisional in comparison to "He" (Jesus), for, ultimately, it ought to concern us most what He thinks of us, our words, thoughts, and actions. Our "theys", can be a source of stimulation, stability, and needed perspective in the midst of hectic, everyday life.

Let us each have the courage, then, to ask: "Who are my "theys?" Why do "they" matter to me in such a special way, and what does this tell me about myself?" And whose "they" am I, and what can I do to respond adequately to that individual?"

One university has a tradition of the "Last Lecture," to which eminent scientists and scholars are invited. The format apparently calls for them to speak of their experiences in their discipline as if this were to be their last lecture. Presumably, this format can induce a discipline that calls for the distillation of weighty comments rather than trivia and for a summational style of speech in which things get said that otherwise would not be "risked."

The analogy is useful in several ways. While one could not always approach tasks or relationships as though this were the "last" opportunity to deal with them, nevertheless, there ought to be more occasions when we deal with each other using eternal perspective. What might a father say, for instance, if this were "the last family home evening?" What would a teacher do and say if the pending lesson were to be the "last" he or she would give this particular class? Too often we withhold the things from others which would be more cherished because we are reluctant to talk about "the things of most worth" and what we have learned in life though pain and sacrifice. Saying things as if they were the "last" can also give authenticity to our relationships with others, especially with the young who crave (more than we know) the communication of cherished things which often go unsaid because we are too casual and because we assume we have an abundance of time. In fact, in addition to the interruption of death, many of our relationships with others are "temporary" and come to an end because of non-terminal events (moving, change of jobs etc.) before some of things that should have been said, or done, got said or done.

There are many scriptures which are less used, less "advertised," than others, but which speak out to us, nevertheless. For instance, in Ether 10:11 it is said of Morianton the king that, "he did do justice unto the people, but not unto himself because of his many whoredoms. . ." How often do we see those in life whose "public" contributions are significant, who treat others better than they treat themselves in terms of doing what is right? History seems replete with examples of men whose contributions were superior, but whose lives contained some fatal flaw which kept them from making even greater contributions and, more importantly, kept them from mortal happiness and from working out their salvation.

Neal A. Maxwell

Some shrug off these defects as being insignificant alongside their accomplishment (which no one can take from them). And since one can hardly measure present misery, and can scarcely measure misery retroactively, rebuttal is difficult. Yet, is it not reasonable to suggest that the maxim, "no other success in life can compensate for failure in the home" was operative then as well as now? Conversely put, "disorder in the passions is mirrored by disorder in the state."* Personality and politics are inevitably intertwined.

In 2 Nephi 32:9, as Nephi nears the giving of his parting testimony, he shares a life lesson with us:

". . .that ye must not perform any thing unto the Lord save in the first place ye shall pray unto the Father in the name of Christ, that he will consecrate thy performance unto thee, that thy performance may be for the welfare of thy soul."

So often we feel, implicitly, that we are doing God a favor if we do his work, that we are helping him along when, in fact, our performance properly undertaken is for the welfare of our soul, not his! It is our happiness and our growth he seeks! How wonderful it could be to pray that what we do would be mindstretching and soul-expanding. Such genuine, prayerful forethought could also reduce the less-than-necessary tasks we do that are trivial and could lessen the number of right things we do for the wrong reasons.

---

*Time, September 19, 1969 p. 71.

_____

Jacob, in 2 Nephi 9:41, in speaking of the straight and narrow, reminds us that "the keeper of the gate is the Holy One of Israel" and that Jesus "employeth no servant there." The emphasis rightly is on the fact that Jesus "cannot be deceived." There is another dimension of reassurance, too: not only will the ultimate judgment not be delegated in order to serve the purposes of divine justice, but also divine mercy can best be applied by him who knows these things what only he can know—the quiet moments of courage in the lives of his flock, the un-noticed acts of Christian service, the unspoken thoughts which can be "credited" in no other way, except through perfect judgment. All of this is good for us to remember in a Church with divine doctrine and divine authority, but with imperfect members who must speak and act for God, though their judgment, unlike His, is imperfect.

The depth of God's commitment to free agency can be seen in many ways. Two little-appreciated examples occur in Alma 1:17 and 30:7,11. In the context of describing how lying was punishable when proved, but, ". . .the law could have no power on any man for his belief," dissent and difficulty were a "great trial" to the faithful, and they "bore with patience the persecution which was heaped upon them." Later chapters described how if a man did not believe in God "there was no law to punish him"; there was "no law against a man's belief." Korihor taxed the patience of the people with his anti-Christ preachings but "the law could have no hold upon him." Korihor's tragic fate and his ironic demise are not common to anti-Christs but we would do well to emulate the forebearance of some of our ancient brothers and sisters.

Those of us who are asked to believe "backwards" (nearly two millenia) in the atonement of a Christ who came and redeemed man may forget the challenge of faith for those whose task was to believe forward—"the worship of a being" who was to come "many hundred years hence." The unbelievers never let our predecessors forget the difficulties inherent in fashioning such a faith prospectively. (See Jacob 7.) Even when the accuracy of the prophecies of early prophets ought to have entitled them to a hearing, the rationalization of unbelievers was, "Some things they may have guessed right among so many." and their excuse was the introduction of alleged geographical favoritism: "Why will he not show himself unto us as well as in the land of Jerusalem?" . . .a "land which is far distant, a land which we know not." It is significant that Jesus did show himself to those on this continent, just as it is significant that we who live now have a more recent array of witnesses who saw Jesus in our own time.

Among the conceptual contributions of the Book of Mormon are concepts such as a definition of a saint:

"For the natural man is an enemy to God, and has been from the fall of Adam, and will be, forever and ever, unless he yields to the enticings of the Holy Spirit, and putteth off the natural man and becometh a saint through the atonement of Christ the Lord, and becometh as a child, submissive, meek, humble, patient, full of love, willing to submit to all things which the Lord seeth fit to inflict upon him, even as a child doth submit to his father." (Mosiah 3:19.)

And again such unique contributions as the concept of "the sorrowing of the damned":

"But behold this my joy was vain, for their sorrowing was not unto repentance, because of the goodness of God; but it was rather the sorrowing of the damned, because the Lord would not always suffer them to take happiness in sin.

"And they did not come unto Jesus with broken hearts and contrite spirits, but they did curse God, and wish to die. Nevertheless they would struggle with the sword for their lives. (Mormon 2:13-14.)

How often one sees individuals trapped in a kind of psychological no man's land wherein their misery seems to suspend them between former behavior in which they can no longer find pleasure and true repentance which could bring them real joy. The ambivalence of those who "wish to die" but fight to live, who "curse God" but deny his existence is prototypic of many modern "hang ups."

Surely the mothers and fathers of today can identify with Lehi's description of himself as a "trembling parent." (2 Nephi 1:14.) All would-be disciples would do well also to ponder the concept of "the man of Christ." (Helaman 3:29.) The lamentation of Mormon who had "led" and

39

"loved" his people "many times" (Mormon 3) (whose discouragement with his people caused him to record, candidly, that his prayers for them were finally "without faith," because of the hardness of their hearts) is a classic case in leader-follower relations. Finally, Mormon refused to lead a corrupt people and stood "as an idle witness" to manifest his disapproval to the world.

Some portions of the scriptures are always relevant; it remains for us to "feast upon the word of God" that we may draw upon those verses which have special meaning for us *now*, but to which we did not resonate in time past.

In spite of the necessary editing, the candid personal observations of various Book of Mormon prophets come through. For those of us who find Isaiah less than clear and stimulating, we overlook the cultural barrier. Note Nephi's words (2 Nephi 25:5):

"Yea, and my soul delighteth in the words of Isaiah, for I came out from Jerusalem, and mine eyes hath beheld the things of the Jews, and I know that the Jews do understand the things of the prophets, and there is none other people that understand the things which were spoken unto the Jews like unto them, save it be that they are taught after the manner of the things of the Jews."

That "there is none other people that understand" such writings as Isaiah save it be the Jews should be of some consolation to those of us who receive gladly the verses of Isaiah we do understand, but who have the simultaneous feeling that we are often missing the point.

One cannot shake either the fragments of the self-image of the Nephites which appear in the Book of Mormon when writers describe themselves as "wanderers in a strange land" (Alma 26:36), and as "a lonesome and a solemn people, wanderers, cast out from Jerusalem, born in tribulation, in a wilderness, and hated of our brethren. . . . wherefore we did mourn out our days." (Jacob 7:26.)

A constellation of scriptures tell us of the Adversary's true purpose: "for he seeketh that all men might be miserable like unto himself." (2 Nephi 2:27; 9:9.) The Devil "rewardeth you no good thing" (Alma 34:39), and "will not support his children at the last day" (Alma 30:60), and "he persuadeth no man to do good, no, not one." (Moroni 7:17.)

For those of us who may need to look back to previous times and previous tasks in the Church for a glow of satisfaction, we can ponder with profit the words of Alma: (Alma 5:26.)

"And now behold, I say unto you, my brethren, if ye have experienced a change of heart, and if ye have felt to sing the song of redeeming love, I would ask, can ye feel so now?" (Alma 5:26.)

How do we feel now, today, about the Church, life, and the gospel? While every life has its peaks and valleys, it is not good for us to live in the past, since the application of Christ's teachings can bring us joy now, with its flood of feelings and sense of *joie de vivre.*

41

Neal A. Maxwell

Lest we think that the lot of a disciple is likely to be one in which he comes calmly to the cross and then carries it lightly to his own Calvary, there are the sober words of Moroni, whose efforts to bring about peace illuminated the basic and deep differences between the Lamanites and Nephites (Alma 44) so clearly and with such pathos that Moroni finally exclaimed; "Ye are angry with us because of our religion." It is a reminder of John's words: "Marvel not, my brethren, if the world hate you."

Because the waters of life everlasting all come from the same divine well, it should not be surprising that conceptual similarities appear between the various books of scripture, both at the lofty levels having to do with Christ's mission, etc., and also at other conceptual levels.

In Alma 13:28 we read, ". . .pray continually, that ye may not be tempted above that which ye can bear. . ." While in 1 Corinthians 10:13 we see: ". . .but God is faithful, who will not suffer you to be tempted above that ye are able: but will with the temptation also make a way to escape, that ye may be able to bear it."

In Moroni 8:16 we read Mormon's epistle to his son, Moroni, which contains this spiritual insight: ". . .and I fear not what man can do; for perfect love casteth out all fear." John wrote (1 John 4:18): "There is no fear in love; but perfect love casteth out fear: because fear hath torment. He that feareth is not made perfect in love." .

42

"For the power is in them . . ."

In Paul's epistle to the Ephesians (4:18,19) he speaks of those "who being past feeling have given themselves over into lasciviousness, to work all uncleanness with greediness," while Moroni speaks of a degenerate culture in which the people are "strong in their perversion" and "delight in everything save that which is good" and are also "past feeling." Nephi observes (1 Nephi 17) that individuals thus sated are "past feeling" so that they cannot "feel" the words of God or his prophets.

The cosmological "case" of Alma (Alma 30:44), ". . .all things denote there is a God; yea even the earth, and all things that are upon the face of it, yea, and its motion, yea, and also all the planets which move in their regular form do witness that there is a Supreme Creator," is strikingly like the Doctrine and Covenants 88:42-47 in its description of the heavens whose order prompts pondering: "Behold, all these are kingdoms, and any man who hath seen any or the least of these hath seen God moving in his majesty and power."

Too seldom do we use the case study approach to the scriptures. When there are sufficent longitudinal data, "portal to portal" persual is high in its yield. Contrast the relationship of Jacob and Esau in Genesis, chapters 27 and 33. We read first how Esau "hated Jacob" and wished to slay him. Years later we read of a moving, tearful reunion in which the same Esau who resented Jacob's portion says "I have enough, my brother; keep that thou hast unto thyself."

―――――――――――――――――――――――――――――――

This tenderization of both men (and give Esau full credit for going the second mile) no doubt contributed to the later full spiritual development of Jacob, but not without Jacob's reaping the consequences of his visible favoritism toward Joseph, which caused Joseph's brothers to "hate" Joseph so much that they "could not speak peaceably unto him." The longitudinal look serves us well again, however, for we finally see the patriarch Jacob blessing all his sons in a full reunion as he approaches death. Then we are given a tender, moving verse which says "And when Jacob had made an end of commanding his sons, he gathered up his feet into the bed, and yielded up the ghost, and was gathered unto his people." (Genesis 49:33.)

. . .In the book of Helaman a phrase is used, "The man of Christ." It is a phrase which capsulates some of the intent of those who wrote in this book. And this part of Helaman's writing says:

"Yea, we see that whosoever will may lay hold upon the word of God, which is quick and powerful, which shall divide asunder all the cunning and the snares and the wiles of the devil, and lead *the man of Christ* in a straight and narrow course across that everlasting gulf of misery which is prepared to engulf the wicked—

And land their souls, yea, their immortal souls, at the right hand of God in the kingdom of heaven, to sit down with Abraham, and Isaac, and with Jacob, and with all our holy fathers, to go no more out." (Helaman 3:29-30; italics added.)

That really is the simple message and expectation we generate. To paraphrase the language of a popular song, "On a clear day the man of Christ can see forever." The gospel gives us the chance and perspective to see forever in terms of what mankind and our mission are all about, and how vitally important what we do with and to each other is. If we can see forever, it is crucial that we not complicate that clear vision nor make the passage of life more difficult, either by complicating the gospel or by failing somehow to keep that simple picture before us.

There is, in the 32nd chapter of Alma, a pleading from the prophet in which he asks us to "give place" in our lives for the message of Christ. To me the test for each of us, in terms of how well we are doing in giving place in our lives, is to ask ourselves, "How congruent are we with the life of Christ in terms of our thoughts, our deeds, and our behavior?" This congruency with Christ is a reflection of what the Prophet Joseph said in one of his lectures on faith when he indicated that when one has really begun to grow spiritually, he will have an assurance that God approves of his life and the direction of his life, not finally and fully, of course, but sufficently that he begins to resonate and respond to the pleadings of God's spirit in such a way that he can have that kind of inner assurance.

When we have congruency with Christ, it means we have to shed everything about us that is inconsistent with the pattern he has set for us. Once we have congruency with Christ, to comply with the standards of the Church is easy, in the sense that it is what we want to do, not what we must do; duty becomes a delight. Congruency with Christ would mean, for instance, that we would consider, in a way we have never considered before, the impact of our behavior on other people—to use the jargon of the young generation, the realization that simply "doing our own thing" is not enough, for when we do "our own thing" we have impact on other people, and sometimes negatively. It may be that we are pure and innocent in what we do, but our actions can be misread by our colleagues and associates and can damage or harm their faith. The gospel suggests, and certainly Paul articulates this well, that we must avoid those things that would shake the faith of others needlessly.

Congruency with Christ means also doing positive things that the ordinary person wouldn't think of doing. Congruency with Christ, in effect, means that we have a kind of inner gyroscope which marks (even more precisely than any printed set of standards or any handbook can do) the path the Lord would have us pursue.

One of the ironies which is fostered, at times innocently, in the Church, is the feeling we have that the spirit of the law is superior to the letter of the law because for some reason it seems more permissive or less apt to offend others. The reverse is true. The spirit of the law is superior because it demands more of us that the letter of the law. The spirit of the law insists that we do more than merely comply superficially. It means, too, that we

46

must give attention to the things that matter most *and still not leave the others undone.*

Notice Paul's counsel to the members of the Church on how to deal with someone in the Church who had erred and the importance of forgiving.

". . .Lest perhaps such a one should be swallowed up with overmuch sorrow."

". . .Confirm your love toward him." (2 Corinthians 2:7,8.)

"Confirm your love toward him." That is strikingly the same as the 121st Section of the Doctrine and Covenants, where we are asked to "increase" our love towards him whom we have reproved. To "confirm" and to "increase" are simple, central, and consistent because the water comes from the same well.

There is in the Book of Mormon a statement in which the Lord says, "Behold this is the gospel, which I have given unto you," and then he describes his gospel. (See 3 Nephi 27:13-18.) It is a simple story of a world to which a Savior has been sent whom men may accept or reject, but who is, nevertheless, the Messiah.

That simple story is the very thing, of course, the world cannot accept, and it is so simple that some may even be offended inwardly at times by the so-called simplicity of the gospel. Jacob, writing in the Book of Mormon, says of the Jewish people who preceded us and who rejected Jesus, that they "sought for things that they could not understand," and that they were forever "looking beyond the mark." (See Jacob 4:14.)

Neal A. Maxwell

───────────────────

The Jewish people, prior to the time of Christ and at the time of Christ, rejected the gospel, in part because it lacked adequate intellectual embroidery. The message was not sufficiently complicated or politically pretentious. Neither was Jesus when he lived among them. There is a kind of theological blindness to which Paul refers in terms of the message of Jesus when he says that to the Jews, Christ was a "stumblingblock," to the Gentiles he was "foolishness."

In many ways, this is how we are situated today. There are those who may share some of our beliefs and values, but for whom the restoration of the gospel is a stumblingblock they cannot get over the top of. But to most of mankind, what we proclaim is "foolishness."

The Book of Mormon tells us more about something we learn of first in the Old Testament, when the children of Israel were bitten by the serpents in the deseret. The Book of Mormon gives us an amplification about the staff or rod upon which those who were bitten had simply to look and they would be healed. And then the Book of Mormon makes this terse statement—it's really an understatement:

". . .And because of the simpleness of the way, or the easiness of it, there were many who perished." (1 Nephi 17:41.)

It is true today; the simpleness, the easiness of the gospel is such that it causes people to perish because they can't receive it. We like variety. We like intellectual embroidery. We like complexity. We like complexity at times because it gives us an excuse for failure; that is, as you increase the complexity of a belief system, you provide more and more refuges for those who don't want to comply. You thereby increase the number of excuses that people can make for failure to comply, and you create a sophisticated intellectual structure which causes people to talk about the gospel instead of doing it. But the gospel of Jesus Christ really is not complex. It strips us of any basic excuse for noncompliance, and yet many of us are forever trying to make it more complex.

The Book of Mormon suggests a third reason why we may like complexity and reject simplicity, and that is because complexity is pleasing to the carnal mind. It gives us sanctuaries for sin.

There are other reasons for craving complexity. One is our simple lack of courage in facing our own deficiencies. The Book of Mormon uses this terse phrase:

". . .The guilty taketh the truth to be hard, for it cutteth them to the very center. (1 Nephi 16:2.)

Most of us don't like to be cut to the center, and when the gospel standards cut us it hurts. The tendency is to deal with the pain by rejecting the surgery.

* * * * * *

Neal A. Maxwell

There should be no Mormon Massadas,* but, in addition to Carthage, there were Haun's Mill and many other times and places forebearers gave everything they had. This past is a part of me which I cannot renounce, even if I fail to be worthy of it.

It is difficult to have a sense of the future without also having a sense of history. Too often we in the Church pick up the trail of the Kingdom in this the last dispensation only with the events of July 24, 1847. Nauvoo is there in our memory, to be sure, but it is a fuzzy image, and the places and events of our people prior to that are even fuzzier in the minds of most members—save the events of the sacred grove in 1820. Our lack of general awareness of what happened at Haun's Mill; or the quiet success of, for instance, Dan Jones, a Welshman, who may have been the greatest missionary of our age in terms of aiding in the conversion of numbers of people (about 4,000 according to Wendell J. Ashton's research); or of the consummate courage of the "Hole in the Rock" people can rob us of both the humility that history can bring and also of the

*Masada (or Massada) was a fortified town on the south end of the Dead sea where the Jews, after the fall of Jerusalem, made their last stand for three years against 10,000 Romans, ending around 72 A.D. The Zealots killed their wives and children and committed suicide rather than surrender to the Romans who, were greeted by a solemn stillness and an awful silence as they finally entered the fortress.

cultural connecting links we have which can spur us on as we meet our own rendezvous with history.

The proud heritage of our Jewish brothers is, even now, a major force that holds together tiny Israel as it acts out a drama, the significance of which many of the actors do not even sense. We have over-reacted to the telling of pioneer stories by a cessation of any story telling in too many homes. Adam and Eve's examples with their children in which they, during their equivalent of family home evenings, shared everything that could be shared, made "all things known unto their sons and their daughters." It is hard to know "where" we are if we are only dimly aware of "who" we are. The ancient Spartans left us a vision that is a more precise analogy than Massada. Outnumbered by the Persians, according to legend, the Spartans had to hold the pass at Thermopylae. After failing to take the pass, the Persians sent an emissary to the Spartans, who asked them to surrender and threatened them by saying that the Persians had so many archers they could "darken the sky with their arrows." The Spartans replied: "So much the better, we shall fight in the shade." We, too, may need to hold the pass in the shade of vexing circumstances; and we, too, need to be undaunted, but that is easier to do, if we carefully cultivate a realistic sense of destiny.

The ebb and flow of cultural epochs in the Book of Mormon shows clearly that when an age had reached its apogee of affluence, there ensued a giddy, moral weight-lessness which seemed to cancel out the very heroic traits

51

which had been hewn from the rock of the circumstances and which produced the moral triumphs so short lived. Seeing the sad, repetitive pattern, one is struck with the possibility that this paradox may be true also with individuals. Only God's insistence on being a perservering schoolmaster, refusing us respite lest it produce relapse, seems to save some of us from being hoisted on the petard of our own performance.

Man is too provincial to fashion any new morality which is true morality. For just as atheism is too simple, man's mortality will always bear the stamp of his environment and the imprint of his particular problems; the response cannot be whole, because man is not whole in his perspective, in his experience, or in his love. He may make facsimiles, using the real morality as a model, but the flaws in his counterfeits are fatal and detectable for anyone who cares about the real thing.

In watching the old, good-natured but unsuccessful struggle to recall a face or fact, one is reminded that whole societies seem also to need to wait for the wheel of memory to come round again as they heedlessly repeat the errors and omissions of the past.

Robert Brustein has brought to our attention a quotation of Plato which seems to appropriate for our time in terms of how the adult generation can unintentionally do the youth a disservice by "throwing in" with them too quickly, too totally, or too carelessly, abandoning the adults' authoritative insights or experience. It is a pattern of some professors in our time. Plato said:

"In such a state of society [a state of democratic anarchy], the master fears and flatters his scholars, and the scholars despise their masters and tutors; young and old alike; and the young man is on a level with the old, and is ready to compete with him in word and deed; and old men condescend to the young and are full of pleasantry and gaity; they are loth to be thought morose and authoritative, and therefore they adopt the manners of the youth."

We need whenever we talk about relevancy, to make allowance for at least some of the restlessness of young people—in and out of the Church—because of the fact that they are in a period of time when, as Bruno Bettleheim observes, youth are undergoing, to some extent, "the empty wait for real life." This waiting can produce boredom, anxiety, and guilt. Yet constant involvement with the gospel in action at any age in life can reduce those very problems because the gospel is always relevant to our personal lives; it does not wait on the granting of a degree or the passing of a birthday to become germane.

The heightened quest for relevancy is no doubt a function of the seeming "human predicament" that has been underscored by the wave of existentialism (produced by the events of our time) which has washed over us. Perhaps people a century ago asked themselves about the relevancy of the activities of their own lives. Chances are, with a

53

few notable exceptions, they were too busy surviving, harvesting crops, coping with the challenges of life, etc., to be unduly concerned. Some sense of history is very important, therefore, in looking at this matter of relevancy. It is vital, too, to distinguish between the significance of saying, for instance, that an organization is irrelevant and saying its membership ought to be doing more.

What follow are a number of observations, obviously not inclusive, which show the relevancy of the teachings of Jesus Christ for our everyday lives—here and now. The fact that there are those who preach these same teachings without seeming to be aware of their relevancy does not reduce the relevancy of these concepts for the perceptive member. By the same token, the fact that many of us fail to apply these teachings in a relevant way in our relationships with our fellowmen does not reduce either the relevancy or the validity of the teachings for those who do apply them.

There is much discussion today about the many faces of alienation. This concern is appropriate, because there are forms of "alone-ness" which are not only inimical to the individual, but which may adversely affect his relationship with the rest of society. The isolate can become a tragically catalytic man as he works out his hostility. This fact was first weaved into the tapestry of truth in Genesis, when it was observed that "it is not good for man to be alone." While this reference related to the significance of marriage, it also is a statement of truth which goes beyond that point of reference.

The Word of Wisdom, whose validity has been demonstrated amply by science—at least in some of its specifics—has too often been lauded solely as a health code, which, while true, often leaves out the relevancy of this doctrine in terms of the awful arithmetic of alcoholism, for instance. If, as many of the young generation maintain, violence and death are the ultimate obscenity, alcohol is obscene in terms of the death and maiming it causes on the highways, the child beatings, and the terrible tragedies in the homes where it visits its full afflictions.

The relevancy of work—the inherent dignity of work with its implicit potential for assuring us that we are needed, that we can influence some things, in an age of boredom and leisure—may need to be restated in fresh terms. An excess of leisure can set in motion forces whose consequences have yet to be fully measured psychologically. The inherent difficulties that often occur around the crisis of retirement are ample, added proof about the meaning of work in our lives. It may even be that we shall live to see the time when there are meaningful "make-work projects" to provide "spiritual" income such as were once used to provide economic income.

Nor have we realized the "insight-lead" we have been given in the message of the Master in terms of how we can best help people and still preserve their individual dignity. Too many stereotyped speeches about the evil of the dole have probably blinded us to the tremendous truth that underlies these urgings to avoid the creation of a dependency relationship which can deny the recipients both dignity and real remedies, ultimately causing failure for recipients and resentment on the part of the benefactors who feel their efforts were unappreciated.

As the Church becomes worldwide, the relevancy of Jesus' teachings can be seen in the way in which these teachings can transcend nationalism and dissolve the differences of boundries and borders. These cross-cultural happenings between Church members are not perfect executions of ecumenicism, to be sure, but they are sufficiently operative in a regular way to remind us of this relevancy and that members can care enough about the gospel to—in the words of Alma—"make place" in their lives for this kind of brotherhood even with their nation's traditional "enemies."

Note this passage in the 49th section of the Doctrine & Covenants, verse 20:

"But it is not given that one man should possess that which is above another, wherefore the world lieth in sin." This ought to remind us of the role that economic disparity plays in causing and maintaining sin, in the grand and tragic sense of the word, because of the envy, the strife, and the greed with all their train of consequences that flow from the cheek-by-jowl relationship of riches and poverty.

In the brief stipulation of virtues to be possessed of men to be elected to public office it is difficult to improve on the relevance of the scriptures which counsel us to seek out individuals who are "wise," "good," and "honest."

Too often we settle for one or two of these virtues only to be disappointed by acts which arise from the absence of one of the virtues in this triad. Each virtue is crucial, as history attests.

We have not yet sensed fully the singificance of King Mosiah's words in the 29th chapter of Mosiah concerning the need in a free society for a balance between the individual's rights and responsibilities; nor, indeed, have we successfully seen the relevancy of the concept of "equal chance." (Read Mosiah 29:33, 34, 38.)

We have probably not fully extracted the relevancy of Joseph Smith's concerns about the quality of life in a city or town where people come together. Perhaps the Mormon villages are not economically viable today. But there are lessons to be learned from Nauvoo. The people of God have often been nomads as well as pioneers, but now we must learn to be urbanites, since we are no longer an ecclesiastical enclave. But we need to reflect on the noteworthy features of the Mormon village in its human-sizedness, the sense of personal accountability and responsibility to the community which too often are lost in a megalopolis.

We often miss, too, the significance of the open-endedness of the gospel. The Taylorian truth of the 13th Article of Faith in which we are urged to be eclectic in our search for and adoption of truth from whatever sources, stands as a monument to relevancy as well as to the intellectual security offered by true spirituality.

There are many ultimate issues which illustrate the relevancy of the gospel. The pile of secular papyrus and paper on which multitudes of men have, for ages, sincerely etched their ideas about the nature of men and the universe ought to be a subtle reminder to us of the relevancy of knowing who we are and why we are here. The special knowledge imparted in the revelations does not automatically make us better or our behavior better—but it could, and it does in the lives of some. We are so close to profound truths about man and the universe that we have let them become trite utterances.

One cannot help but admire the cosmic optimism of some humanists and existentialists even though they are, in terms of man's ultimate destiny, pessimists. But we ought to have the added thrust and drive that are born out of knowing that there is a plan for man and that immortality is not an idle speculation or an opiate. Spiritual knowledge of that kind should not only comfort us at the time of funerals, but should also give our day-to-day relationships with each other more meaning and richness. Since we will be together a million years from now, we should develop our friendships with even greater care, candor, and love than if we knew each other only as functions in a brief encounter.

God has leveled with us in terms of who we are and what our priority tasks are. The overarching gospel truths about life and purpose are tremendously germane, but we are so close to these truths that in our failures to exploit them, we are like the early natives of Utah who froze while sitting on beds of coal.

"For the power is in them . . ."

One is aware of at least some of the impasses that can occur, at times, in an individual's interface with the institution of the Church. The analogy of the importuning widow is appropriate in that its message about change within channels, redress in the right way, may be worth some reflection by the younger generation. Some of the learning we are intended to receive can grow out of those impasses. For instance, that it was not simply that Laman and Lemuel needed to learn from their model little brother, Nephi, but that Nephi had to learn some of life's important lessons by learning to cope with Laman and Lemuel. We cannot, for instance, limit our chances to do good to those formal calls to action that come from the Church and be true to the spirit of the 58th Section of the Doctrine and Covenants, verses 26-29. The statement of the First Presidency of September 7, 1968, is an added reminder of the obligations we have to enrich and to shape our contemporary environment. We can brood because our favorite civic or political issue meets with silence on the part of some in the Church, or we can do our part individually.

The gospel itself reminds us that God leaves terribly important tasks to what seem to be terrible ordinary people. Human frailties in a divine Church cannot help but produce mood swings in some of us. The human parts of the Kingdom are bound to produce, too, such things as morality fads among some of its members. It is inevitable that we see in the Kingdom those who preach well but live poorly in terms of the spiritual significance of their lives, as well as those who live well spiritually but

59

whose powers of articulation are not adequate; they know and do much more than they can say.

Youth will find life confirming the relevancy of the gospel with its revelations, if they are willing to risk living by them while they are yet in the process of validation and while they are in the very stage of life when they could be drawn off by the counterfeits that exist for each and every basic tenet of the gospel. Youth can err, too, by "specializing" in the Church, in that they focus too much on one aspect of the gospel, punishing verbally other members for their failures to see it their way. If youth do this, though their cause may be just, they are no more right than the ardent genealogist who buries himself in the archives while Rome and home burn.

As youth and adults read the scriptures for relevancy, we should remember:

1. There are some scriptures that are a recitation of facts that describe former situations. These may be interesting in an informational way, but not in a salvational way (i.e., the dimensions of the ark, though these were very relevant to Noah if he wanted to keep dry).

2. There are some scriptures which hold "hidden treasures of knowledge," which will become particularly relevant later on, depending on our willingness to search the scriptures to meet those needs when there is learning readiness.

3. There are some scriptures that are relevant to us *right now*—that can sing to us now the song we now most need to hear!

4. There are other scriptures that provide rich historical and spiritual data and insights on a longitudinal basis about individuals or groups (such as Moroni 9 or Ezekial 16:49).

It is our individual responsibility to develop a congruency with Christ by avoiding the compartmentalization which would reduce the relevancy and joy of the gospel in our every-day lives. The insights in the scriptures can help us cope with, conceptually and behaviorally, the very deficiencies we have, if we can trust enough to try. Peter facilitated his personal growth and helped nonmembers by his willingness to accept revelations, even if reluctantly, pertaining to those who were then "outside" the system—the Gentiles. That Peter showed some equivocation later in life may be true, but he courageously and clearly made much more progress than would otherwise have been possible if he had not opened himself to the changes which the gospel wrought in him.

Ponder, if you will, the possible significance of those scriptures that may speak of our particular time when they speak of an age when the earth shall be in commotion, and men's hearts shall fail them, and the love of many shall wax cold. Events can shake us, bring on despair, and cause us to shrivel up in our capacity to love—unless we have *faith and love* based on truths that are relevant not only now but in eternity! We may become bearers not only of revealed truths—but of that precious needed commodity, hope, which significantly is part of that triad of truths—faith, hope and charity—without which nothing else is really relevant!

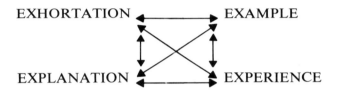

EXHORTATION ← → EXAMPLE

EXPLANATION ← → EXPERIENCE

To be effective in creating learning situations and to be effective in leading, all four of these ingredients are needed if we are to improve behavior in ourselves and in others. Our homes, our classes, our quorums should provide all four of these ingredients. If we are defective in our emphasis on any one of the four, it is my judgment that that "shortage" occurs with regard to "experience."

We provide too few opportunities beyond-the-classroom which can let us "feel" and "see" the truth and the joy of the Gospel. So much of our time is spent with the lecture part of our Gospel curriculum that we do very little planning and executing with the "laboratory" part of our Gospel learning. We see many examples where parents provide exhortation and explanation without example and experience. We see occasional leaders who provide example without explanation. It is vital that we maintain a tension balance between all four ingredients of learning if we are to be fully effective and if we are to witness for ourselves—intellectually, experientially, and spiritually—that the gospel is true and that it does bring blessings beyond compare! We can say this best when we have "tried the experiment of its goodness!"